Stretching
Exercises for Guitarists

D1554681

ISBN 978-0-9569547-9-4

Written by Gareth Evans

Cover design and adaptation by Gareth Evans

Technical advisor Jan Evans MCSP. Grad Dip Phys

Illustrations by Chris Evans

www.guitar-book.com

Disclaimer: The information provided in this book is intended for information purposes only. You must not rely on it as an alternative to medical advice from your doctor or other professional healthcare provider.

You should consult with a doctor or healthcare professional before starting any exercise, or if you have or suspect you might have a health problem. If you have any specific questions about any medical matter, you should consult your doctor or professional healthcare provider. You should never delay seeking medical advice, disregard medical advice or discontinue medical treatment because of information in this book.

Contents

Why Stretch?

Connective tissue holds us together by connecting and supporting different types of tissues and organs in the body. Fascia is a type of connective tissue that binds parts of us together, or separates them in sheets enabling them to slide smoothly over each other in movement. Fascia surrounds nerves, blood vessels and muscles, and is also interwoven between muscle fibres (myofascia). At the end of muscles, the surrounding sheets of fascia come together and concentrate to toughen and form tendons, which attach the muscles to the bone by blending into the bone, becoming part of it.

Fascia connects many different parts of the body. Because of this, poor posture in one part of the body can lead to pain in another. For example the nerves and blood vessels in the neck supply the shoulders and arms, so if the neck is held in poor posture this can contribute to pain in the shoulder(s), elbow or wrist.

The most vulnerable spots are where nerves pass through junctions of movement, such as through the shoulder joint, elbow or wrist. The carpal tunnel is a narrow passage in the wrist, through which several tendons pass to the hand and fingers from the forearm muscles. The median nerve (which supplies sensation to the palm, thumb and all fingers but the little finger) also passes through the carpal tunnel. This is a lot through a relatively small space, so repetitive movement and strain can take its toll. It is important to keep supple and healthy by not overdoing anything, and using stretches and mobilising exercises.

Stretching is good for you because it mobilises the fascia keeping it freely moving. Stretches should not be held for too long, but should be done intermittently for short periods. A single sustained stretch would not allow the circulation to return to the parts being stretched, and tissues' flexibility can only build up gradually or be maintained with intermittent stretching.

If you have stiff muscles, a heat-pack or wheat bag placed on the problem area can help relax the muscles and increases circulation. A hot bath can have a similar positive effect for stiff muscles, particularly larger ones such as in the back, shoulders and neck.

"An ounce of prevention is worth a pound of cure"

(Benjamin Franklin 1706-1790)

Playing Guitar

How you hold your posture while you practise and how you practise are important factors.

Be sure your guitar is the right size and comfortable for you. When reading music, use a music stand set at a comfortable height. This should be with the middle of the book at your eye level as you sit upright. The distance should be close enough that you don't have to lean forward too far in order to see it. This may depend on your eyesight, so if you require reading glasses, using them can also benefit your posture.

For the human body, like anything with moving parts, movement can be good for us, even a simple walk, keeping us limber and the fascia supple. Being fixed in the same position for a prolonged period of time is not ideal. With extended practise we tend to build tension in our neck, arms and hands, so when practising guitar it is a good idea to change posture every now and then. For this you could practise between being sat down and stood up, also changing the knee on which you rest the guitar can help.

When stood up to play it is best to have the strap at least high enough so that the guitar is the same height on you as it would be when you are sat down; this way your playing technique won't require adjustment. Having the guitar slung too low isn't particularly good for posture

because it can make your back and neck bend forwards, which increases the angle of the wrist required for the fingers to reach around the fret-board.

As you begin to play start simple and slow, leaving more taxing playing for later on. Have patience and don't play constantly without taking small breaks of 10 to 15 seconds every now and then, and take short breaks of 3 to 5 minutes between every 20 minutes of playing. Always pay attention to your body and hands; if it hurts then stop, if it starts to become a strain or feels as though it is about to, then take a short break.

This also makes better guitar practise; if playing for too long your hands can become tense then you lose control over any fine movements required for whatever skill level you're at, and you will not improve. A short break can make a notable difference in your ability, rather than attempting something over and over again.

When pressing down on the frets, use only the amount of pressure necessary to produce a clear sound and no more. Being aware of this is better for the hands, and in the long run can make more tricky and faster playing easier. Stretches can also loosen up the fingers allowing you to make more intricate and quicker movements on the fret-board.

Last but not least regular physical exercise enhances your performance and improves cognitive function, as does a good diet.

Stretches

The stretches in this book are divided into several sections: the Neck & Shoulders, the Back, Nerve Mobility, Forearm, Wrist & Fingers, and Fingers & Thumb. From the Forearm, Wrist & Fingers section onward, some of the stretches start with an easier version, then more difficult. Only do the ones you are capable of and are comfortable doing, so if that is the easier version then that's all you need to do. Don't try to do any of the exercises in this book any further than you feel is comfortable. If you can't stretch as far as shown in any of the illustrations this is not a problem at all; stretching within your limits is more effective.

Overall posture when doing all of the stretches should be with the chin in so that the earlobes are vertically aligned with the shoulders, while the shoulders should be gently down and back. Your back should be upright.

Find what exercises suit you (you don't have to do them all!) at the time of writing this I do 1.1, 2.1, 2.4, 2.5, 3.1, 3.2, 4.2, 4.5 and 4.7 most days of the week.

1. Neck & Shoulders

1.1 Neck Retraction - This counteracts the forward head posture that can develop in musicians. Tuck your chin in gently and pull your head back gently. Hold this for 3 to 5 seconds. Repeat 6 to 10 times. This is best done while sitting upright.

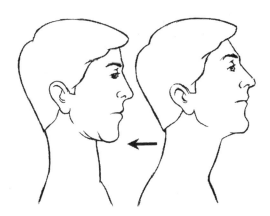

1.2 Backward Shoulder Rotation - Rotate shoulders backward 6 to 10 times to loosen up shoulder joints and open up the chest. Rotating backwards is better than forwards because it opposes bad forward posture in which the shoulders are hunched forward.

Finish the exercise by drawing your shoulders down and back to strengthen the lower trapezius muscles, which stabilise your shoulders.

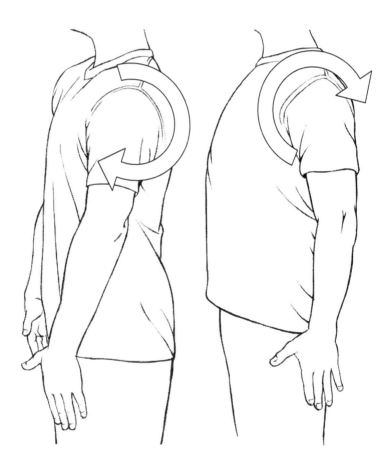

1.3 Doorway Chest Stretch - Place your forearms on the door-jambs either side as shown in the picture. Gently lean forward to stretch the pectoral muscles across the front of your shoulders and chest. Hold for 3 to 5 seconds and repeat 6 to 10 times.

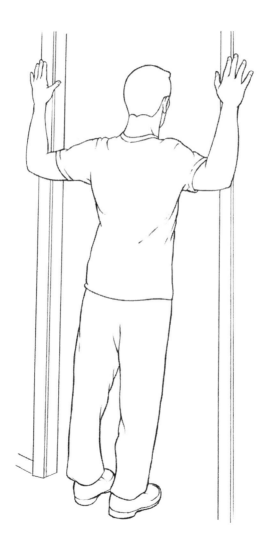

2. Back

2.1 Upper Back Rotation - a) Sitting with your feet firmly placed on the floor, hold your arms out in front of you horizontally with one forearm resting on top of the other. b) From a central position, rotate briskly to one side then return back to the central position. Repeat 6 to 10 times.

This is a spinal rotation exercise, best done in the opposite direction to how your back is held as you play. If you play right-handed your back tends to be rotated to the left as you play, so this exercise is effective if done to your right. Vice versa if you play left-handed.

a)   b)

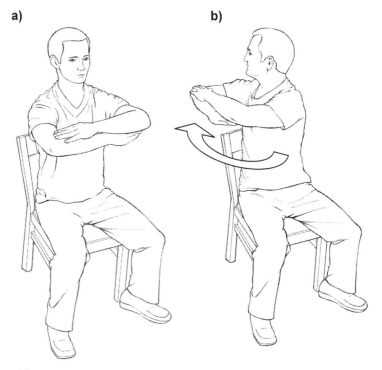

2.2 Lower Trap & Lat Wall Stretch - This stretch is for the upper fibres of the Latissimus Dorsi back muscle and the Lower Trapezius; normally tricky muscles to stretch as they are primarily stabilising muscles.

Stand beside the door-jamb and hold around it with one hand. You should not be in the doorway but to the side of it so that if someone were looking through from the other side they would only see your fingers. Place the foot that is furthest from the wall behind the other foot out to the side (cont. overleaf)

Pull your body away while using the elbow of the other arm to push on the door-jamb to provide resistance in order to localise the stretch to the upper back. The following picture illustrates this from above.

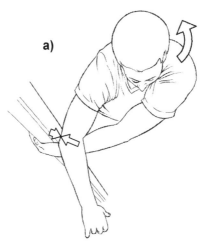

a)

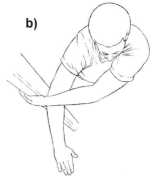

b)

You can place the resisting elbow above (a) or below the stretching arm (b) to alter the angle of the stretch.

This stretch works on the parts of the back that can be prone to over-use in guitar players, as the muscles remain statically contracted while you hold up or reach over the guitar, and can become tense with sustained playing. If you are right handed then your right side back will be more affected, and vice versa.

2.3 Side Stretch - Sit upright on a chair. Put one arm over your head and gently bend to the side reaching down with the other arm. Hold for 3 to 5 seconds and repeat 6 to 10 times.

2.4 Upper Back Stretch I - If you have been sitting with a guitar for a while it can affect your upper back. This is the stiffest area of the back and often becomes even less mobile with a sustained position.

Lean backward over the back of a strong enough chair with your arms folded behind your head and hold this position for 6 to 10 seconds. Repeat 3 to 5 times. Putting a towel or cushion behind your upper back can help. This stretch extends your back the opposite way that it would have been while playing guitar.

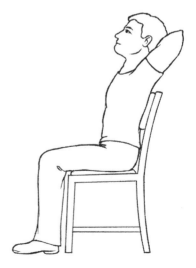

2.4 Upper Back Stretch II - Using a device such as a back stretcher can effectively stretch the joints in your spine. A back stretcher with rollers enables the vertebrae to separate and stretch the spine naturally.

Gently lower yourself onto the back stretcher, and relax there for a minute. Don't stay on it for too long initially; you can gradually build up to 10 minutes over time. Back stretchers will come with their own instructions.

The back stretcher has been demonstrated to be effective at stretching the spine in the following research paper:

James W. DeVocht et al. Biomechanic Evaluation of the Rola Stretcher as a Passive Distraction Device Journal of Manipulative and Physiological Therapeutics Volume 23 • Number 4 • May 2000

2.5 Back Rotation - Lie down with your arms out on each side and knees bent up. Lower your knees to one side with your head turned to the other side. Hold this position for 10 to 20 seconds then repeat in the opposite direction. Repeat the exercise 3 to 5 times.

This exercise is good for your back and also stretches your arms and sides. If done with your knees more bent, as above, the rotation takes place in the lower back.

If done with your knees less bent (as shown on the next page), the rotation takes place further up your back.

3. Nerve Mobility

Nerves coming down from the neck connect to all the muscles and supply sensation to your shoulders, arms, hands and fingers. Inflammation from over-use can become a problem for nerves particularly at movement junctions such as the shoulder, elbow or wrist, where they can become caught up or stuck.

Therefore they need to be kept mobile with gentle exercises to maintain healthy nerves that can move freely amongst all the tissue they pass through.

3.1 Median Nerve Mobilisation - Hold one arm out as in the picture below with your shoulder down and back and thumb pointed back.

Keeping your shoulder down with the arm rotated outwards and thumb pointed back, gently extend your elbow and wrist. Extend only as far as you can until you feel reasonable tension in your arm, forearm or hand. Hold for 3 to 5 seconds then release back to the previous position. Repeat this exercise no more than 6 times and no more than twice in a day, as nerves are sensitive.

3.1 Median Nerve Mobilisation II - Doing the same exercise with both arms puts more tension on the nerves and is slightly more difficult.

Hold for 3 to 5 seconds then release back to the previous position. Repeat this exercise no more than 6 times and no more than twice in a day, as nerves are sensitive.

3.2 Radial Nerve Mobilisation - Hold one arm as in the picture below with your shoulder down and arm inwardly rotated with elbow bent.

Keeping your shoulder down, slowly straighten your elbow and bend up your wrist and fingers until you can feel reasonable tension in your arm, forearm or hand. Hold for 3 to 5 seconds then release back to the previous position. Repeat this exercise no more than 6 times and no more than twice in a day.

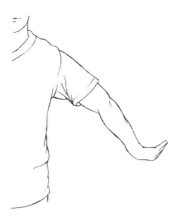

3.2 Radial Nerve Mobilisation II - Doing the same exercise with both arms puts more tension on the nerves and is slightly more difficult.

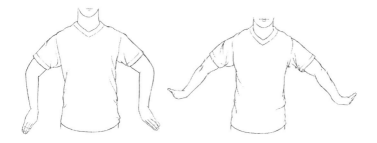

Hold for 3 to 5 seconds then release back to the previous position. Repeat this exercise no more than 6 times and no more than twice in a day.

4. Forearm, Wrist & Fingers

4.1 Forearm & Hand Massage - Massage the forearm and hand muscles to increase circulation and relax them.

Outside forearm
(Extensor muscles)

Inside forearm
(Flexor muscles)

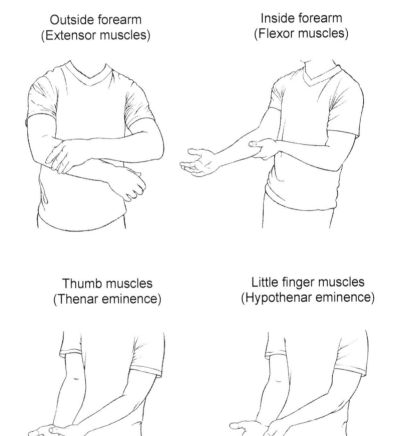

Thumb muscles
(Thenar eminence)

Little finger muscles
(Hypothenar eminence)

4.2 Forearm Extensor Stretch I - Hold an arm out straight in front of you and bend the wrist and fingers towards you using the other hand. Hold for 3 to 5 seconds and repeat 6 to 10 times.

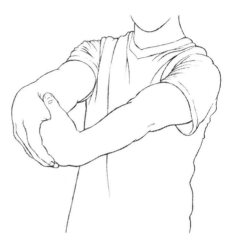

4.2 Forearm Extensor Stretch II - A trickier version. Rotate the arm inwards while holding it out straight in front of you. Bend the wrist towards you using the other hand making sure to keep your elbow straight. Hold for 3 to 5 seconds. To stretch and release just bend the elbow a little and then straighten it to stretch again. Repeat 6 to 10 times. This is also a useful stretch for Tennis elbow.

21

4.3 Forearm Flexor Stretch (Ulnar Nerve included) - This exercise also gently mobilises the Ulnar nerve, which supplies sensation to the lateral side of the hand, little finger and half of the ring finger.

a) Hold your hands together in front of you in the praying position making sure your forearms are horizontal and in line with each other.

b) Maintaining this position move your arms to the side as shown in the picture. Hold for 3 to 5 seconds and repeat 6 to 10 times. Do this in both directions.

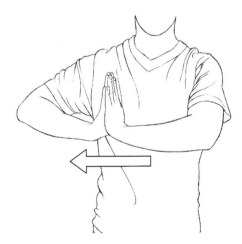

4.4 Wrist Flexion Stretch - This will stretch your wrist joint. Hold around your wrist with the thumb and middle finger of the other hand, and use the palm to press down a little on the back of the held hand and let your elbows go down naturally. Hold for 3 to 5 seconds and repeat 6 to 10 times.

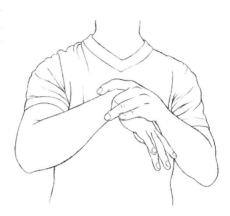

4.5 Wrist & Finger Stretches - The main muscles that operate your fingers are in the forearm, so in order to fully stretch your finger and wrist extensors and flexors, your arms should be straight. With your arms straight and downward in front of you, bend the fingers / wrist as shown in the pictures.

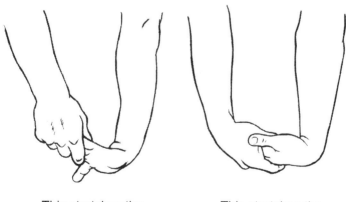

This stretches the wrist flexors.

This stretches the wrist extensors.

23

4.5 Flexor Stretch II - A slightly more difficult version of the flexor stretch is to hold the arm straight and start with the palm facing downwards then bend your fingers and wrist back, as follows.

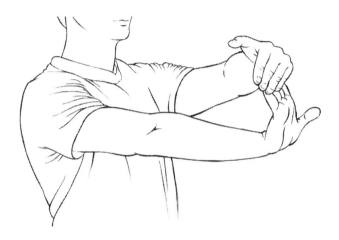

4.5 Flexor Stretch III - A little harder again is to hold the arm straight with the palm turned upwards then bend back the fingers and wrist with the other hand.

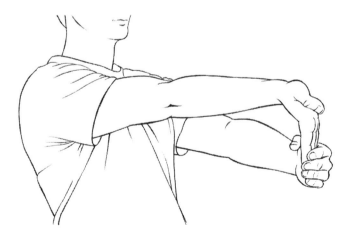

4.5 Flexor Stretch IV - Here is a quick stretch you could do while playing the guitar. The stretch may look far in the picture but make sure only to go as far as you are comfortable, and don't hold for more than 5 seconds.

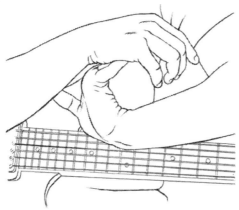

4.6 Finger, Hand & Wrist Stretch - With one forearm upwards hold the fingers back with the other hand in front as shown in the picture. Hold for 3 to 5 seconds and repeat 6 to 10 times.

4.7 Hand Shake - Moderately shake your hands. This is good for circulation to the muscles and ligaments after they have been held in a set position while playing the guitar.

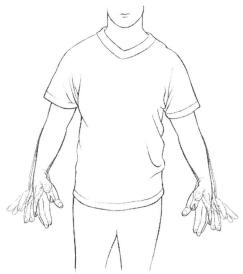

When shaking hands have your arms either downwards or upwards above your head. This is because shaking is an uncontrolled movement. If the arms were held out horizontally there would be extra gravitational force to add to the force of the shake when going in the direction of the floor. Shaking with the arms up or down makes it less likely to jar your wrist(s).

4.8 Wrist Rotation - While gently holding one forearm stable, rotate your hand at the wrist in one direction a few times, and then in the other direction a few times. Repeat for the other hand.

(Pictures on next page)

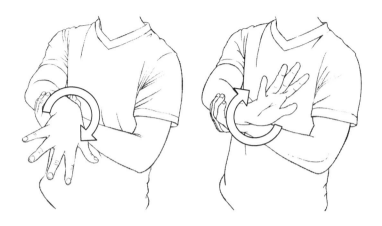

5. Fingers & Thumb

5.1 Finger Stretch (into extension) I - To increase mobility of individual fingers, with an arm held straight, hold back a finger while using the thumb behind the knuckle to stabilise, as shown in the picture. Hold for 3 to 5 seconds and repeat 3 times for any one finger. Use on each finger as required.

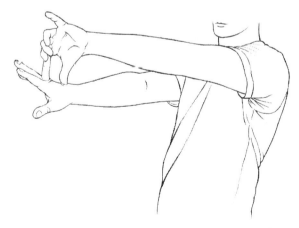

Moving the free fingers about while one is being stretched is good as this is similar to the independent movement of the fingers on the guitar. This can be applied to the following two finger stretches also.

5.1 Finger Stretch (into extension) II - A slightly more difficult version similar to Finger Stretch I but with the hand held the other way up as shown in the picture.

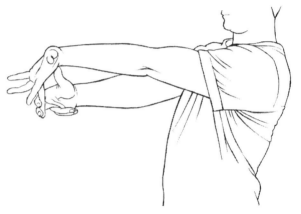

5.2 Finger Stretch (into flexion) - Push a finger into flexion by using your thumb as shown in the picture. Hold for 3 to 5 seconds and repeat 3 times for any one finger. Use on each finger as required.

5.3 Inter-digital Stretches - Use the thumb and a finger / fingers of one hand to stretch between the fingers of the other. Hold for 3 to 5 seconds and repeat 3 times between each pair of fingers as required.

The finger independence required on the fret-board isn't only down to the coordination of your fingers but also their individual strength. Elastic bands placed around pairs of fingers, which you separate against the resistance of the elastic band can be used as an exercise to build up this strength.

5.4 Thumb Stretch (Carpus & Saddle Joint) - This opens out the palm and stretches the small joints in the wrist at base of the thumb. Hold a hand out in front of you with the thumb pointed away as shown in the pictures. With the other hand, hold the base of the thumb with the fingers while using the thumb to apply counter pressure on the knuckle of the middle finger. Hold the stretch for 3 to 5 seconds and repeat 6 to 10 times for each hand.

5.5 Thumb Joint Stretch - This stretches the thumb joints. Using the same position as in the previous stretch, hold the thumb from above as shown in the picture.

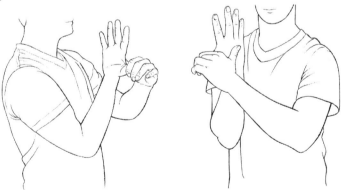

5.6 Qui Gong Balls - Two iron balls of about 1.5″ in diameter that you circulate around each other in your palm. You could try it clockwise and counter clockwise, one way will be harder than the other.

This flow-like motion of the finger joints with minimum force makes the hand muscles feel smoother and is good for repetitive strain injury. This can also be good for your hand if you use a computer mouse, as are stretches 1.1 and 2.4 if you sit at a computer.

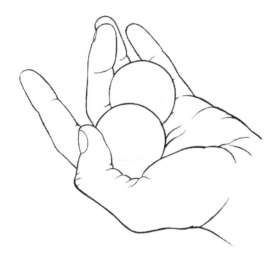

Other books by this author…   www.guitar-book.com

Made in the USA
Las Vegas, NV
30 November 2023